KEIRA HOPE

Love Letters in a Forgotten Box

You can find more from Keira Hope on social media
@keirahopewrites

First edition

This book was professionally typeset on Reedsy.
Find out more at reedsy.com

Contents

III   Fragments

IV   Denouement

Dedicated to Mr. Martin — Who sparked my love for all things literature and poetry. If it weren't for your class, this book would not exist. Thank you.

I

Love Letters

to lightning bugs

I wonder if fireflies look up at the storm and see themselves —
  Lightning flashes through the night sky, momentarily illumi-
nating the world in white and purple,
  and I imagine the fireflies watch in awe.
  Soon, a chorus of them glow yellow,
  lovingly mimicking their namesake.

to lady death

What is life if not a kiss?
    Tell me not of work — where has that gotten you?
    Laying on your deathbed, will you reminisce on time behind
a desk?
    You cannot take it with you
    No, instead be surrounded by family
    Remember only the riches of consequence

A melody kisses your ears
    Her sweet song, a parting breath
    She asks you a final question
    Will you waste your last words with regret?

I will tell Her about the feeling of paint on my hands
    The warmth of sunlight on my skin
    The taste of sweet nectar lingering on my tongue
    While you lecture about a thousand monetary things

No, tell me not of your menial tasks
    I'd rather listen to a mother hum in the kitchen
    Or feel the glistening cold of the lake water in spring
    For life is not something given, but something made yourself

No, She will not praise you for your years full of empty slaving
  Work without passion is like a mother without child
  And a life without love is not a life worth living

to old friends

What remains after we're gone?
   life, touched by the life of others
   an imprint, an impression
   values imbued or love taken
   a silhouette of something stolen

I still carry with me
   the lives of old strangers
   infatuated with memory,
   people they used to be
   in some far corner of my brain
   collecting dust in a keepsake box

but now all that remains
   is the goodness that you gave me
   and the people I've yet to love

to broken teapots

don't fret, dear
  a handle down and still you pour
  lift others up, but your lid is no more
  engraved and carved, yet you stand strong
  work some more, it won't be long

don't cry over the life that you won't live
  it's not your fault your maker was weak
  broken down, and still you breathe
  your body cries while you pour tea

drip drop, one cup down
  a thousand more, but don't you frown
  hide your cracks with steady hands
  fill you up till you can't stand

pressure builds and still you pour
  tea seeps through your cracks and onto the floor
  they'll say the flood was sudden even as you shatter
  falling to the ground, your broken pieces will scatter

don't fret, dear

in the earth you were born
you'll be turned back to clay
to be formed once more

to new life

A gift from mother nature
  Fruit, bent down from her boughs
  Sweet gift, full of life
  Bring life anew to those around you
  To watch you grow
  What was life like before?
  I've found my purpose in loving you

to the moon

One night, I sung to the sky:
   Sweet moon,
   Why do you cry?
   I see your tears that fall as moonbeams on the land,
   And the puddles that are born from your eyes.

A shooting star is your only emissary,
   Carrying a message that most cannot read.
   But *most* are not like me;
   They do not hold my understanding.

So I plead to thee:
   Give over your plight to me,
   And find that I know very well
   The shadows in which you dwell,
   And I say, you're not as far away as you seem.

to my soulmate

Are you out there, love?
  The one my soul was forged to embrace?
  Do you search for me,
  in the first morning breath that you take?
  When the sun wakes up and paints the sky in beautiful hues,
  do you study them relentlessly?
  Hoping you'll see me, like I do for you?

In each note, imbued with passion,
  Do you listen for my voice?
  Do you sing a little louder, hoping your song will bring me
joy?
  Do you pray that your melody will carry,
  and seep into my ears?
  And send with it your love,
  so I know that you are near?

Though you've never seen me,
  Do you paint me like you have?
  Like you know every inch of my skin,
  and every scar on my back?

When you look up at the night sky
   and trace my face in the stars
   Do you make constellations in my name?

Do I feel just as far?

Lost on lonely nights,
   does your bed lay cold and bare?
   Vacant save yourself, and fantasies that are not there?
   Or can you feel me beside you, craving for your touch?
   In the small hours of the morning,
   do the empty dreams become too much?

And on those often lonely nights,
   do you start to wonder why
   it's crumpled, empty sheets
   and not me by your side?

When the days grow stale
   and devoid of any color
   Do you grow weak, like me?
   and let your mind start to ponder...
   if I ever existed at all?
   Or if maybe your soul was forged alone
   left, forgotten, on the table
   with no match to call its home

to myself

I think I like the way I look after a long day:
    the way my hair bunches up in my hand as I comb out the
tangles,
    and how my slightly-smudged makeup softens my face.
    I like the way my worn clothes sag gently over my frame,
    and I like the paint covering my hands.
    I think I could stare at my reflection for a long time;
    and I think I deserve it too;
    The world is harsh and rough,
    but my reflection is mild and soft

to the universe

There's a certain humanity in not understanding,
   in acknowledging and accepting the ever present unknown,
   in wearing that gap,
   between all that we know and all that we don't,
   like armor, until we no longer need that protection,
   when, in death, we understand.

to —

overcome with longing,
   tearful and indignant,
   wrought with aches and trembling —
   thoughts, alone and terrorizing,
   I am plagued

II

Free Verse

from the box, #2

For as long as I can remember, there has been a warning sign
in the back of my head
   my subconscious trying to send me a message
   but my mind is on fire and I can't see through the smoke

The weight of the would-be words sit heavily over me
   like a looming storm cloud before it shatters
   always lingering, I wait for the hammer to fall

I've never given much thought to destiny
   I'd rather trust the journey to lead me where I'm meant to be
   I know someday I'll have to accept the truth that sits heavily
   but for now, I dream of better days
   perpetually pondering the premonition in the smoke.

the burden of the mystery

ravenous—
    the desire, intrinsically deep
    wound tight with the string of my soul
    to capture life
    flowing through all things

from the box, #3

and How can you not love life?
   You, who sees the world as cruel and unforgiving
   Must be blind to miss the love around you
   As blatant as the sun

reverie

When my head disconnects,
    It floats, almost gently, away from my body
    Soaring upward through the clouds
    Untethered and uncontrolled

My thoughts fall out on the ascent,
    Scattering through the air like feathers from a beaten pillow
—

    Mere parts of a whole,
    Worn and useless, caught helplessly in the wind

My body, blind and deaf,
    Must venture out to capture them
    And tie them to the dirt ridden earth
    So that in the morning,
    My feet may feel the soft caress of verdant grass
    As I stumble through the field
    To collect my head
    From the warm meadow where it landed

hollow bones

Youth, tender ache
  Hollow of my bones
  Shadow cast behind me,
  left me long ago

My temple — once cherished
  Its walls now creak in the wind
  wood worn to paper,
  shaken in the mildest of storms

The storms come now often
  They rattle these old bones
  Wash through me like the tide
  and take from me unknown

I stand on the rocky cliff
  as eroded as my frame
  Yearning for something —

seeds

Like the petals of a dandelion
   floating softly through the air,
   I break —
   and dissolve into pieces,
   taken gently by the wind,
   to sprout in the spring

lungs

and I think, that's what it's like — to be alive
   to let the words tumble off my tongue and out into the world
   afraid not of where they came from nor where they land
   to let them pass gracefully between you and I,
   or none-so gracefully,
   rather they be clumsy
   their meaning all the same
   The air will clog with feeling,
   rich and unnamed and new,
   neither wish to brand it so
   for fear of chasing away that moment that sits so delicately
in our presence

home

Often,
    I wonder about home.
    How long can I stay away before I can no longer return?
    I'm not confident I know where it is anymore.
    For so long I was quite sure, but five years have passed and
time has blurred most certainties.
    Am I home now?
    Or is it still a thousand miles away,
    waiting for someone who will never come back?

I left a piece of me behind in Vermont.
    I think I dropped it somewhere in the mountains,
    and it grew into this tree —
    tall and looming and ancient,
    and something so subtly me.
    The branches stretch far above,
    and the trunk is carved with a name.
    Hikers will walk by and wonder who I am,
    or maybe they won't think anything at all.

I think that piece of me is gone forever,
    but I can almost feel it still, like a phantom —

and if I focus enough, I can feel the wind rustling the branches,
and see the valley I once knew so well.

I lost a piece of me in California, too —
    I think I lost a lot more than that —
    but mostly I think it fell off at the beach,
    or maybe the waves eroded it out of me.
    Now I can feel the tide, as old as the moon,
    and I can hear the waves and the kids playing in the sound,
    even when I'm stuck on land.

I wonder, also, if I lost a piece of me here,
    and where exactly it fell off.
    I don't think I'll realize it until I'm gone, and it's far behind
me.

I wonder where else I'll drop pieces of myself, to become one
with the earth,
    and I think, maybe,
    that's home —
    that maybe you have to lose a little bit of yourself to find your
way back.

pine

I let the feelings grow like fungus on the forest floor,
   spreading and flooding, blooming and light
   until my body is consumed in flowers,
   and how rapidly they sour!

They shrivel and they blacken,
   their moldy bones spread,
   deep into my lungs,
   thorns piercing my veins

Until my blood is red and wet on the ground,
   and dark petals droop and wilt,
   decaying and decomposing,
   everlasting in that shallow grave

insomniac

I can't sleep with an unwritten poem on the tip of my tongue —
    it writhes in my mouth,
    thrashing against my lips and teeth and straining the muscles
in my jaw,
    but I can't always capture it on the page.
    If I force it, it'll cut up my cheeks and I'll smother it until it
dies weakly on paper,
    but if I leave it I think it'll smother me too;
    there's a balance that I haven't quite learned,
    of leaving it to ruminate, tormented in my mouth,
    long enough to form fully so it can survive outside of it,
    but not restraining it so long that it destroys me too.

eighteen

The year eighteen always smelled sweet in my mind;
   A faraway dream, ripe and vibrant and hazy,
   like a mirage in a desert,
   as if, in my head, my whole life could come down to that one
year, filled to the brim with experiences.
   But it was always just that —
   an illusion, a heat dream: dust in the wind, distant and wavy
and intangible.

I was never meant to *be* eighteen,
   but to look at it from afar and admire it, to study its content
from behind a glass;
   to consume it and paint it in my memory,
   but that cage was never meant to be opened.

I worry that I'll waste that year, that sweet eighteen,
   and I remember how sweet seventeen sounded too;
   and I see the broken glass, cage open,
   painting ripped to shreds...

momentclature

The moon was as full as my heart,
   Glowing and round and opulent,
   And I remembered, a long time ago,
   Someone told me I would crash my car because I was looking
at the moon.
   I laughed, as I drove ten miles an hour through the parking
lot, staring up at the sky
   And the memory faded into the sunset behind me.

I'd like to leave lipstick stains on all my things,
   And stare at the moon,
   And laugh at myself as my makeup runs down my face in the
shower.
   I want to remember — the moments,
   Past and present,
   Painful and pleasant.
   I want to live in the small minutes alone,
   To chip away at the gnawing nihilism and form my life from
what's left.

october

I felt a loss — something I never had.
  its absence echoed loudly in the hollow confines of my chest.

ode to aphrodite (reprise)

They call it greed, or lust —
   that wanting, intangible,
   infinite and undefinable,
   in every waking moment.

It floats around me,
   smokey and choking,
   and it fills my lungs to bursting.

Aphrodite calling,
   I, alone, must answer.
   She speaks, that voice
   to my ears, melodic in tone,
   enchanted, wicked under her control.

I am completely at its mercy;
   breathless and wandering,
   aimlessly, asunder in love
   Solely one thing can sate it,
   which I have not yet found.

november, fellow of my heart

November, fellow of my heart
   Companion of change
   Season's turn, usher in the unfamiliar
   Through the dark, your path alight
   No one knows your guidance like I

So often overlooked
   Chill mistaken for malice
   But your breeze bids us shed our hair
   To leave behind overgrown belief
   For something sweeter

You nurse that infant flame
   So meek within my soul
   To a passion so bright, threatens to consume
   You'll tame it yet, with whipping wind
   Refine that excruciating beauty
   Into soft pleasure

November, I bid thee well
   No one knows my soul like you
   When eternity passes,

And I am morphed beyond recognition
I'll hold no fear
Only your tender guidance

saint of devotion

That land that stretches out between me and thee —
    unyielding and infinite in its separation,
    will by my hand become passable,
    that one day we will reunite.

here lies an artist

Mostly, I just want to be known
  So I impart my soul however I can —
  on paper, with words,
  or on canvas, with paint.
  I don't know if it works,
  if they understand me at all,
  but I like to think that someday
  when my body is long gone,
  someone will find my things and say,
  "Here's someone a little like me."

III

Fragments

neither here nor there

i.

a supernova, burn bright and quick
  gone in the blink of an eye

ii.

art pours out of me like a crack in a reservoir
  a new river forged, but it leaves me empty
  a hollow shell to get washed away in the stream

iii.

sit safely at home and watch the snow-speckled sky
  there's a thousand more stars on a winter-kissed night

iv.

candle light flickers from within, casting each carving in a
sinister glow

v.

once a muse is captured, what is it worth?
    a duplicate, a fake, an ill-willed copy

vi.

chest open, heart beating on the floor
    blood seeps into the cracks in the wood like sap flowing
through the veins of a tree
    turn the fluids flowing out into a sickly sweet treat
    the door's open

vii.

strife strides into the cool night
    fiery words disperse under the starry sky

viii.

that infinitesimal essence
    sought and wrung out on the page
    ethereal translated in desperation

ix.

when — not if — the love fades, worn by time and distance into
something akin to bitterness
    it'll eventually give way to that soft knowing, deep in my soul,
that I, in loving you, however brief
    became a better version of myself

x.

my garden of words
    surround me in greenery

xi.

I haven't changed much at all
    time will sit me down one day,
    in her room on the edge of the universe
    and we'll catch up like old friends.

xii.

my love, forged into a pearl in my chest
   taking up space in my heart like a tumor
   buried in the bottom of the ocean
   please, won't you take my pearl away from me?
   promise you'll take good care of her
   and the empty shell she leaves behind

xiii.

how can you bear that cynical view weighing on your shoulders?
   I can't stand to watch you waste our lovely, limited time here
on trifles
   yet my pleas fall on deaf ears

xiv.

run, then
   deep into the woods
   I'll sing to the birds instead

xv.

I'm tied, to another
   and she calls me,
     from gray working day
     to the wild afar

xvi.

in another life,
   I'd be a dancer:
   taken by the music,
   married to the stage

xvii.

traverse the heavens momentarily, so far from
   earthly dwellings,
   but every time I must fall,
   briskly, back to the ground
   the descent as breathtaking as the crash,
   air stolen from my lungs,
   as I fall back into my earthly problems

xviii.

let me yearn, honestly and relentlessly,
   with all that I am

xix.

I think I'd follow you anywhere —
   even if I had to take a train to the edge of the night sky,
   and collect every piece of stardust to
   put you back together.

xx.

if asked what we talked about,
  I think, most appropriately, I should say,
  "everything" —

xxi.

I so love how words change —
  it's *my* city because I love it,
  I call my hometown not by its name but by "mine" because
  I loved it once, and that love never really leaves
  because loving is a little like possession, and you change when
you're loved

xxii.

and I felt like I had to have something taken from me –
  ripped from my veins,
  to feel loss as an afterthought,
  emptier again

xxiii.

once fleeting moments
  return at the forefront mind
  sweet impermanence

xxiv.

the past — a painting
    sits at rest on the mantle
    a window, untouched

IV

Denouement

the box

My life lives inside my head:

It's a drooping box — that could certainly use some more packaging tape on the seams — made of worn cardboard with a little bit of water damage.

The sides are covered in scribbled writing — red and black and blue, and the flaps are haphazardly closed, slightly bent, and it's a wonder the thing has survived so many moves.

I couldn't tell you what's in the box —

not for a lack of wanting, but truly,

I don't know what's inside.

If I had to guess,

there'd be old photos,

dozens of slightly blurry snapshots, probably printed at Rite-Aid, with my grandmother's scrawl on the back in permanent marker detailing the year.

It's old birthday parties, mostly, and a family reunion or two.

But the photos are always in the summer — the sun would bleach the film a soft yellow, and solar flares would decorate the sky like fairies, and then there'd be me:

three, four years old, with my dad's sunglasses sitting on the bridge of my nose, way too big for my face above a smile just as wide,

at five or six, donning floral pink outfits adorned with
watermelon stains to match the ones on my face,

in third grade, playing out in the woods with my cousins,
various twigs held tightly in my too-small arms,

just before middle school, picking apples, when I knew
everything and held not a care in the world for the dirt on
my knees or the fruit in my crooked teeth —

the photos would probably start to dwindle, after that.

I'm not sure what else the box might contain.

Maybe a laptop, brimming with childhood stories I never
finished writing,

or maybe blank postcards I never sent,

and, maybe, a list of all the things I ever said.

I don't know, exactly.

Maybe the box is half empty,

waiting to be filled,

while I'm loitering beside it, looking for more tape

author's note

I started writing poetry seriously in the latter half of 2023, during my senior year of high school. The first poem from this collection that I wrote was "to lady death," (initially called "Untitled." I know, so original). I then got a vision of a little box, hidden under one's bed, filled with unsent love letters, and the idea for this collection was born. Every poem in this book was written from August 2023 - October 2024. It's like my own bittersweet time capsule. Each poem is indicative of a very specific feeling I felt at a moment in time, and these poems are like a vessel for me to look back — and now you all can too.

I want to give some special thanks to some special people: firstly, to my parents, who have always been my biggest supporters, especially with this project. My mother has been begging me to get this book out into the world for ages, so y'all have her to thank for reading this. And my dad too; who has always understood my peculiar creativity in a way no one else has. I want to thank my wonderful friends who have been reading these poems over the years and giving me words of encouragement. I appreciate it more than y'all know. Also, I suppose I should thank all of the fleeting infatuations that I had during this period as they inspired many fits of poetic insanity. Some of my best work is thanks to that. Lastly, I want to show appreciation to all of the wonderful teachers I have had over the years that helped cultivate my love for writing — I wouldn't be here without you. Thank you.

about the author

Keira Hope spent her youth pursuing every creative avenue she could, and as a result developed a deep artistic view of the world. She loves to share her perspective in many different mediums, especially through her poetry. When she's not writing, she's probably spending time with her family, learning a new instrument, or looking for cool rocks.